Walter H. Nelson

COMPOSITION IN

PICTURES

COMPOSITION

IN

PICTURES

THIRD EDITION

BY RAY BETHERS

•

PITMAN PUBLISHING CORPORATION

NEW YORK • TORONTO • LONDON

ASSOCIATED COMPANIES: SIR ISAAC PITMAN & SONS, LTD.,

LONDON • MELBOURNE • JOHANNESBURG •

SIR ISAAC PITMAN & SONS (CANADA), LTD., TORONTO

PRINTED IN THE UNITED STATES OF AMERICA

PREFACE

THIS BOOK has now become a standard work, not only for students and professional painters, but also as a university and art school text. In the preface to the first edition I wrote "This book presents many ideas that should prove useful in composing pictures, ideas gained from the universal experience of artists from all time ... But the most important elements in composing any picture are beyond the scope of this or any book: the integration of your own thought, your own personal feeling, and your particular point of view."

This, the third edition, is positive evidence of the validity of the original conception, that of visual comparison between similar compositions, accompanied by concise explanatory text with corresponding diagrams. Drawing, as such, is seldom considered in the pages that follow, for drawing *is* composition just as composition is the *picture*.

This edition expands the sections on color and value and includes notes on the theory of "Passage" and on Abstract Expressionism.

RAY BETHERS
New York

MUSEUMS

Both the author and publisher of this book wish to thank the following museums for their interest and willing cooperation:

Addison Gallery of Art, Andover, Mass.
American Museum of Natural History, New York
Art Institute of Chicago
British Museum, London
Brussels Royal Museum
Cleveland Museum of Art
Detroit Institute of Arts
Frick Collection, New York
Isabella Stewart Gardner Museum, Boston
Louvre, Paris
Metropolitan Museum of Art, New York
Minneapolis Institute of Arts
Museo di San Marco, Florence
Museum of Fine Arts, Boston
Museum of Modern Art, New York
National Gallery of Art, Washington, D.C.
National Gallery, Oslo, Norway
National Preparatory School, Mexico City
Philadelphia Museum of Art
Portland Art Museum, Portland, Oregon
Prado, Madrid
Vienna Museum
Virginia Museum of Fine Arts, Richmond
Walker Art Center, Minneapolis
Worcester Art Museum, Worcester, Mass.
Yale University Art Gallery, New Haven, Conn.

CONTENTS

COMPOSITION IN

PICTURES

"One soon learns that there is no mystery in the fact that things not beautiful to ordinary vision can be made beautiful in pictures. It is nothing more or less than a question of composition—not, of course, arrangement, which is the ordinary photographer's notion of composition; but the artist's ..."

Leo Stein

From APPRECIATION: PAINTING, POETRY AND PROSE, *by Leo Stein* *—through the courtesy of* Crown Publishers

What Is Pictorial Composition?

According to the *World Almanac,* there are 2,150,599,199 people in the world. But why is it that no two of these people look exactly alike? Mothers can always tell one twin from another; and while some people's faces may remind us of others, still, as far as we know, no two people have the same kind of features on the same kind of face.

But since everyone has only two eyes, two ears, one nose, and one mouth, the same elements in similar positions on similar shapes, what is it that makes each face different? Since the "subject" *face* is always the same, it must be the *pictorial composition* that differs, the relation of parts to a unified whole, the varied relationships of size, position, and shape.

As Matisse once said, not about faces but of the art of painting, "It is really and essentially a flat plane with colors upon it arranged in a certain order."

[3]

Composition Can Be Instinctive

The unknown folk painter who created this picture probably never heard of *pictorial composition,* and was obviously not trained in the theory of perspective, color harmony, or any similar phase of the painter's craft. But he had a desire to paint, and did so; it was as simple as that. And it is obvious from his picture that he painted from the way he felt rather than from what he saw. But did he *think* when painting this picture, or did he rely on feeling alone?

Composition Can Combine Both Thought and Feeling

Henri Matisse *thought* as he painted, as his own words indicate. He wrote, "I certainly do think of harmony and color, and of composition, too." But he combined his thought with feeling, for isn't it true that no work of art can be entirely "thought out," but must always be a combination of thought *and personal feeling?*

As André Gide once said about the art of writing, "The most beautiful things are those that madness prompts and reason writes."

HENRI MATISSE: The Window. *Detroit Institute of Arts.*

Art Is Not a Copy of Nature

Since art and nature are not the same, they are each experienced **in** different ways. It is true that painters have been inspired by nature **from** the beginning of time, but any work of art is always made *by* man, *for* man, as an end in itself, and *not as a substitute* for nature.

By comparison with the photograph of the motif, Cézanne's unfinished watercolor *The Bridge at Gardanne* is an excellent example of the creative artist's approach to nature rather than the copyist's.

ERLE LORAN: Photograph of the Motif, from *Cézanne's Composition* by Erle Loran, University of California Press, 1943.

Art Is Not a Copy of Nature

The actual world is always three-dimensional, in unlimited space, while the painter is always limited in his translation to the particular shape of the two-dimensional area he chooses to paint upon. In interpreting his subject in this unfinished picture, Cézanne reduced the proportion of the foreground trees, enlarged the bridge in the middle distance, and greatly increased the size of the distant church. Thus the picture is a combination of what Cézanne saw with how he felt, integrated into a particular format.

PAUL CÉZANNE: The Bridge at Gardanne. *Collection of the Museum of Modern Art, New York.*

Nature Can Be Confusing

Forms seen clearly in the three-dimensional space of nature are apt to be confusing when accurately transferred to a picture surface of only *two* dimensions, as in the above picture. Indeed, it is often the function of nature to be confusing.

But since it is impossible to create *actual* volume or space on a flat plane, a purely artificial spatial method must then be devised to give the *idea* of space where there is no space.

GERALD H. THAYER: Partridge. *Courtesy of the Metropolitan Museum of Art.*

[8]

—but Pictures from Nature Need Not Confuse

Here, in contrast to the picture opposite, natural forms have been translated in three-dimensional space on a flat surface without confusion—an interpretation, but not a *copy,* of forms in the actual world.

RICHARD EURICH: The New Forest. *Collection of the Museum of Modern Art, New York.*

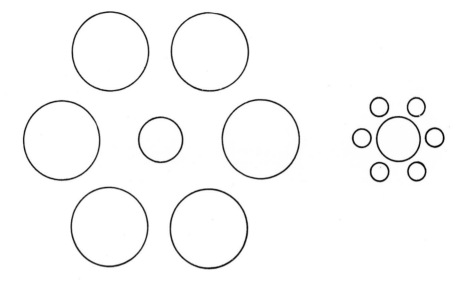

Why Compose?

In any literary work, words necessarily follow in logical order, ideas developing one from another in a sequence of actual time. Music, like writing, is also a time art. But painting is static and without time, a space art with all its elements seen simultaneously.

To give life to this static two-dimensional area, it becomes necessary to create some kind of visual order by controlling the lines, shapes, and directions of pictorial composition so as to simulate time where there is no time.

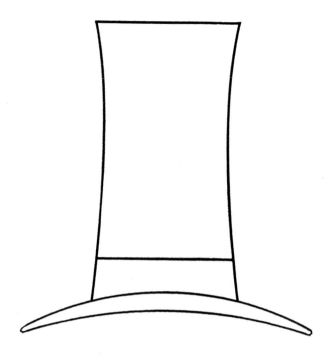

Art and Science

A work of art is always complete, a unified whole endowed with a mysterious quality for renewing itself. It is alive no matter what its age or origin, and is one answer to man's emotional needs. Science, on the other hand, is always incomplete, and answers to physical needs only.

Yet many principles of composition are based on scientific facts, on visual phenomena that an artist can combine with emotional expression in composing pictures. Size, for instance, is never absolute, but relative: as shown by the center circles in the two groups at the left; and the hat, which is actually as high as it is wide, appears taller only because of its particular line *directions.*

Composition and Subject Can Be Separated

While the subject of any picture can be part of the composition, the composition is *not* necessarily part of the picture's subject. This fact enables either one, subject or composition, to be considered separately, as in these two pictures by Lamar Dodd where *one* composition serves *two* subjects in two different pictures.

LAMAR DODD: The Breaker. *Collection of the Pepsi-Cola Company.*

[12]

Composition and Subject Can Be Separated

The seascape on the opposite page was painted, not from the ocean, but from this still life seen in the studio *upside down*.

LAMAR DODD: Still Life (*Shown upside down*).

Composition Can Vary with the Same Subject

Rather than using *one* composition for *two* subjects, as on the preceding pages, Raoul Dufy has here created *three* compositions of varying lines, shapes, and directions, from only one subject.

RAOUL DUFY: Changing of the Guard. *All photographs courtesy of the Carroll Carstairs Gallery.*

RAOUL DUFY: Changing of the Guard at St. James Palace.

RAOUL DUFY: Changing of the Guard, St. James Palace.

Composition Will Vary with Different Painters

Since we see not only with our eyes, but also with our mind, past experience, and personal feeling, it must be true that no two people can ever see the same thing in exactly the same way.

CLAUDE MONET: Sailboats in Argenteuil. *Photograph courtesy of Durand-Ruel.*

Composition Will Vary with Different Painters

These pictures were composed by two painters from the same place at the same time, but not in the same fashion.

PIERRE AUGUSTE RENOIR: The Seine at Argenteuil. *Portland Art Museum, Portland, Oregon.*

Compositions Have Been "Borrowed"

As David Vinkeboons was born in Mechlin some years after the death of Pieter Breughel, there can be no doubt that *The Harvesters* was painted first, and that Vinkeboons later "borrowed" Breughel's composition in painting the above picture.

DAVID VINKEBOONS: Summer. *Courtesy of the Metropolitan Museum of Art.*

Compositions Have Been "Borrowed"

While David Vinkeboons "borrowed" this composition, he also changed it enough to lose much of its spatial movement, pattern, and feeling.

PIETER BREUGHEL: The Harvesters. *Courtesy of the Metropolitan Museum of Art.*

Seeing Will Vary with Different People

In a previous book, *Pictures, Painters, and You,* I endeavored to classify various kinds of seeing and to point out some reasons why we all see so differently, this being true not only of the painter but also of the person viewing his pictures.

The following discussion of "How We See" is reprinted (in part) from this book.

Looking is not always *seeing,* which requires the use of all senses plus past experience. Scanning usually takes the place of seeing with most adults, a casual glance giving just enough information for everyday use.

Sensory impressions are subject to great variation in everyone, with one sense usually dominant. Some people react chiefly to what they hear, and will prefer music to painting, while others will be more responsive to sight, and their preferences will be exactly the reverse. Even where seeing is the stronger sense, hearing, touch and all other senses will be combined in the actual seeing process.

Any picture is always made up of three parts: the artist, the picture, and the observer; all are of equal importance in communication of this kind. The observer will always gain in experience in direct proportion to what he has to give; his capacity to see is almost as important as the artist's ability to paint. To reverse an old saying, "We like what we know"; in other words, we understand what we are looking at.

Seeing can easily be learned, like any other skill. This fact has been demonstrated many times in acquiring knowledge of the relation of mind to sight. Given normal vision, from then on, seeing is primarily a mental process, the eyes acting only as lenses for the transmission of light from the world outside.

To a child, his world is filled with countless *new* things to see, and each one is naturally a new experience. His first view of a tricycle, for instance, with no previous memory of its function, might be only three round forms and some curious angles. Although out of reach, the child will still attempt to reach out and touch it, not yet having learned that depth perception is only part vision, and part memory of having traveled a similar distance before. He then crawls until he can actually touch this new thing; tastes it with his tongue, and bangs it on the floor to see what kind of noise it makes. Then he spins a wheel—a new discovery— and pushes the tricycle along. All these experiences are new and different, and he has discovered them all for himself. It may still be necessary, however, to teach him that a tricycle is made to ride upon. But once he has ridden his tricycle, and learned its name, he will never again see it with the same fresh vision of exploration. From then on, he will see it through use, through its function, rather than in purely visual relationships.

As we all grow up, this fresh viewpoint becomes dulled, and seeing becomes a habit, used for naming things rather than for actually *seeing* them. It remains for artists—who have retained that childlike ability to see things in themselves, and for themselves—to give back to others a fresh viewpoint on things scanned but no longer really seen, of new relationships of form rather than habit relationships of use. Artists do not try to paint what is already seen, but endeavor to point out new ways of seeing.

Seeing has become a habit when the name or use stands for the visual memory of things, or when a specialized interest blinds one to other unseen qualities. To illustrate, suppose our cousin Emma has a new dress, and we prepare to take her picture. We focus carefully on Emma and her new dress, and with the sun behind us, we snap the shutter. But it is only later, when the picture is finished, that we see what hadn't been seen before—the telephone pole which now protrudes from cousin Emma's head. Our specialized interest in Emma and the new dress had prevented our seeing the pole at the time the picture was taken.

On the next few pages, seeing has been theoretically divided into four parts: practical, specialized, reflective, and pure seeing. Not that one kind of seeing is unrelated to another, but this division may help to clarify the way we see. Jan Gordon and Ralph M. Pearson have both written on kinds of seeing, and what follows represents, in general, a continuation of their points of view. [*Modern French Painters*, by Jan Gordon, John Lane, London, 1923. *How to See Modern Pictures*, by Ralph M. Pearson, The Dial Press, 1925.]

Practical Seeing

This is protective, instinctive, the kind of seeing used in quickly stepping aside to avoid being run down by a car. Even lifting one foot after the other in climbing stairs is instinctive, and not usually the result of conscious visual effort and conscious response to a visual stimulus.

Specialized Seeing

Previous interests and training greatly affect this kind of seeing, and can either intensify an image or lessen its visual impression. A bridge of structural steel seen by an engineer, an African chief, and a ballet dancer could hardly appear the same to all three.

How often have we heard the expression, "But it isn't true to nature!" This implies a knowledge of what nature looks like, which, of course, varies with each individual. The bare brown hills of California are considered by some to be very beautiful, but a farmer might prefer green hills—the bare hills, not being productive, would have no beauty for him.

Reflective Seeing

Things remembered condition this kind of vision. Seeing a picture of a barefoot boy with a fishing pole over his shoulder might start a long chain of reflections, such as "Long ago, when we went fishing with Uncle Ben, who met us at the station and drove us to the farm. He had an old dappled mare with a straw hat, how odd she looked," and so on.

A picture, in reflective seeing, does act as a spur to the imagination, but starts a train of thought that may soon have no relation to the original subject. In other words, a glance has been enough to make us remember other things while we forget the picture completely.

Pure Seeing

This is the field of the artist: to see without relation to use, self, or other nonvisual considerations. This kind of seeing does not refer to "what does it look *like?*" but to "how does it actually look?"

An automobile in *practical* seeing is only a menace to life and limb, to be avoided, and is naturally only partly seen in so doing. In his *specialized* seeing of this same automobile, an ignition expert might immediately look under the hood to investigate his real interest, the ignition system, without ever seeing the car as a whole. *Reflective* seeing could bring memories associated with an earlier car of the same make, memories which replace the thing seen.

But *pure* seeing is an experience. No painting, as a work of art, is ever conceived without pure seeing, which cuts through habit, extraneous ideas, and all other restrictive barriers directly to the thing itself.

This automobile, in *pure* seeing, becomes an oblong black form in relation to other curved forms, with discs on either end. In words, this description sounds cold and not very descriptive. But note that it is not in terms associated with other things. This point is significant. Pure vision is used in painting, a visual medium. Pure vision was also used in designing the car itself. But pure vision cannot be used to describe the car in words; reflective or specialized vision translated into words might do it better, for pure seeing is *purely* visual, and cannot be translated into any other medium.

These differences between pure seeing and other kinds of seeing, I think, are the cause of so much misunderstanding in all art criticism: the attempt to translate pictures into words, a different medium of expression entirely.

A Primer of Pictorial Composition

As has been mentioned before, painting is a space art, all elements seen simultaneously, *without* the element of time. It is pictorial composition that channels this simultaneous seeing into an orderly sequence where forms, colors, and directions are observed in some kind of sequential order.

It can then be realized that any discussion of pictorial composition in words cannot hope to approximate this simultaneous effect of pictures, but must follow on page after page over a period of time.

To help in overcoming this conflict of time and space, the next few pages define and illustrate many terms and conceptions used later in discussing the composition of pictures.

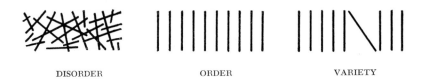

DISORDER   ORDER   VARIETY

Order. Perhaps the first objective in composing any picture is to create *order* out of disorder; but while disorder is confusing, order alone is monotonous without the inclusion of *variety* and *personal feeling.*

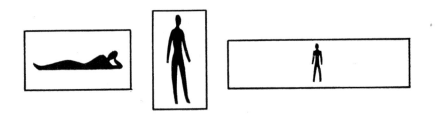

The Format. The format of a picture is its particular shape and proportion; this word is also used to describe size, as large (or small) format.

[24]

The format of a picture should be clearly established at the *beginning* of a composition; for once the shape and proportion are decided, all lines, shapes, and directions will be influenced by the format.

The figures in the left and center diagrams are in accord with their particular formats, but the *vertical* figure in the *horizontal* format is out of relationship, dividing the format's horizontal direction rather than becoming part of it. It can readily be seen that any number of similar lines or directions can be integrated in a picture without confusion if they *relate to the format;* otherwise, as in the third format diagram, they will *interrupt* rather than intensify a dominant direction.

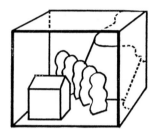
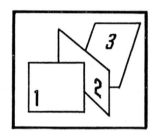

The Picture Plane. The picture plane is the flat surface on which the picture is painted: the plane *through* which the picture is seen, and the plane which by comparison establishes all other lines, planes, and directions in the space behind it. Whereas the *format* is the proportion of a picture, the picture plane is the basis for judging plane directions and for describing two- and three-dimensional space.

The diagram on the left shows pictorial space as it recedes from lower left to upper right, *behind* and in relation to the picture plane, the house as a *cubic volume* occupying *positive space* in *negative* or unfilled space.

The right-hand diagram is a simplification of the plane directions in the left diagram. Plane 1 is without movement or direction; it is *static* in its parallel relation to the picture plane. Plane 2, however, is a *dynamic* thrusting plane, representing the *collective* direction of the five smaller planes (trees). Plane 3 is also dynamic, but is tilted in relation to the picture plane.

In painting, planes are not always definite shapes, but can indicate felt directions without being actually seen.

[25]

Pictorial Space and Mechanical Perspective. Pictorial space (not to be confused with perspective or the illusion of distance) can be demonstrated by an "exploded cube" where overlapping planes are established in space in relation to one another and to the picture plane.

But mechanical perspective is an inflexible system to give the illusion of distance, both by progressively diminishing size, and by making lines converge at vanishing points on the horizon. Parallel lines, as observed in the actual world, do converge; but the perspective system is one-eyed in that it converges far more rapidly than our *two eyes* perceive.

The use of perspective can save time for architects and engineers, but no matter how well any artist understands perspective, the artist and not the system must dominate in composing pictures.

Three Kinds of Space. The space in the left diagram is clearly indicated by planes that overlap in a lower-left to upper-right recession. The center diagram, however, illustrates *confused space* where spatial recession is apparently established by the relative position of the *bases* of the two objects; yet the far object refutes this by overlapping the upper part of the foreground jug. The right diagram shows *equivocal space*, space that can be seen in two ways at the same time. Due to the dual contour of the two objects, the jug, which at one time appears to be far, can at another time be seen on the near plane.

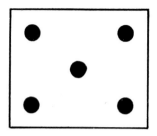 

Pattern. Pattern is two-dimensional and does not destroy the flatness of any surface to which it is applied, but flat pattern alone will not convey the depth of emotion that can be achieved in pictures by the combination of pattern with three-dimensional space.

Pattern is not necessarily restricted to being only geometric, but may also be freely designed, as outlined in the preceding diagram, on the right.

 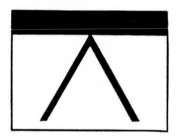

Pattern Combined with Space. This is one of the most important factors in pictorial composition. Where two-dimensional pattern is combined with three-dimensional space, the picture is not only organized in two dimensions on the surface, but also from *front to back behind the picture plane.*

These two simple diagrams illustrate this combination; the diagram on the left is a black pattern on a flat plane, while in the second diagram this same shape can be seen either as flat pattern or as extending back into pictorial space.

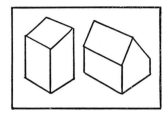 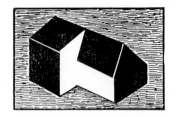

New Shapes from Old. Every great painting is fundamentally an abstraction no matter what its subject may be. But what is an abstraction?

This word has been used in various ways in relation to art, and does need clarification. As used here, it *does not* mean *abstracted* from nature.

The Museum of Modern Art, New York, in *Cubism and Abstract Art,* says: "'Abstract' is the term most frequently used to describe the more extreme effect of the impulse *away* from 'nature'." In other words, as a picture gets further from "nature," it becomes more abstract, becoming, by degrees, a "near abstraction," and when all relation to the world of actuality is gone, it is called a "pure abstraction."

The creation of new shapes from old is an abstract idea, inherent in composing pictures. Two unrelated forms are shown in the diagram on the left; but in the other diagram, these two forms are unified by a *new abstract shape* common to both which did not exist before.

Interval. The *interval* of a picture is the collective pattern of shapes and lines arranged on the picture plane to form an eye track of visual directions, as is suggested by the left-hand diagram. (The term is derived from the *interval* between shapes.)

In the right-hand diagram, however, the star is "out of interval" both by its unrelated geometric shape and by its "out of rhythm" position on the format.

Transparency and Interpenetration. In painting, *transparency* and *interpenetration* permit a "seeing through" from one plane to another, which flattens space and brings it into closer relationship to the picture plane. It is also a method of showing objects in two positions in space at the same time, an effect not shown in this particular diagram.

Subjective Lines. These are simply implied lines to be visually completed by the observer. In this diagram, the larger triangle is only partially suggested, to be visually completed by subjective lines.

Texture. *Texture* in painting can be an actual texture, a roughened surface for instance, or can be simulated by a pattern of lines, spots, or similar indications.

Texture adds new meaning and variety to any color or value, for identical colors will appear different if their textures differ.

The diagram shows four simulated textures in a progressive scale of *five values* including the untextured area of black.

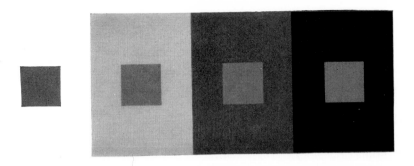

Value. Values are the scale of grays between, and including, black and white. The above diagram shows how a limited range of values can apparently be extended through contrasts, where the same middle value will appear both as a dark against light, and as a light against dark. Any light area (value or color) will also appear larger than a dark one of the same size and shape, owing to its capacity for *reflecting* light.

When any painting depends for its effects on the *value* contrasts of dark and light colors, it is a *tone* painting rather than a painting in *color*. True color paintings are based on color contrasts, perhaps of the same value, rather than differences of dark and light color value.

Tone paintings reproduce quite well in black and white, but the color differences in color paintings are impossible to translate into monochromatic values.

Color. Color is energy; it can affect the human body, mind and spirit. Beyond one end of the color spectrum is infra-red, or heat, while at the other is ultra violet and atomic energy.

Color mixing is an absolute science; it is predictable and can be formulated, but the *use* of color in painting is an art. Colors to a painter are creative tools, used for their emotional effect rather than as parts of "color schemes."

Scientific knowledge of color can help any painter, even though instinct must be his ultimate guide. For instance, it is well-known that warm colors appear to come forward, cold colors to recede. This can be explained scientifically because our eyes cannot focus on two colors of widely separated wave lengths at the same time. Thus, when orange (warm) and blue (cold) are placed side by side, the blue will always appear farther away. Cézanne used this principle in constructing his monumental compositions of volume and space.

Color, for the painter, largely consists of two factors, complementaries and the opposition of warm to cold. Both these qualities are indicated on the small color diagram at the bottom of the page.

This color wheel is based on pigments, rather than primaries of light. In theory, mixtures of these three pigment primaries, red, yellow, and blue will produce any known color, but in practice this is not true. This limitation is due to the chemical impurities in all pigments, so that a chromatic palette will, of necessity, contain additional colors.

But continuing, in theory, a mixture of any two primaries will become the complementary or opposite of the remaining color. These are shown opposite one another on the chart.

Adjacent complementaries will accent one another, and since both appear brighter they have the effect of extending the available color range.

Warm and cold colors also accent one another, but to a lesser degree. Their most telling effect is in the creation of volume and space. The color wheel is divided into warm colors on the left, cold on the right. However, this can be interpreted only in a very broad way, for warm and cold are not absolute, but relative. Certain blues, for instance, which appear cold in isolation will appear as warm against a colder blue. Do not forget that colors are also affected by texture, size, and shape.

Gray, black, and white are not colors, but will accent and clarify adjacent color areas.

It is impossible here to do more than outline the painter's attitude toward color, but if there is one general adage, it is this—

A complex composition will demand simple color, while complex color is best expressed in a simple framework.

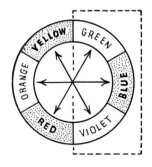

Translating from the Actual World

This is an outline intended to show some differences between the "actual" world and a picture which translates this world of three dimensions into the idea of three dimensions on a flat plane.

These two ideas are somewhat foreign to each other. Movement, for instance, as it takes place in the world of actuality covers a period of time, but as seen in a picture is necessarily static.

The following is a general idea of the difference between actuality and pictures, rather than between actuality and a work of art.

ACTUAL WORLD	PICTURES
Movement	*Movement*
The actual world is composed of movement through space in any or all directions. Movement may be continuous, and part of this may be **only** remembered movement.	A picture is necessarily static, and while action can be indicated, it must be done with the aid of devices such as rhythm, directional lines, arrangement of planes, etc.
Field of Vision	*Field of Vision*
It is possible to be aware of space in all directions. However, in actual seeing, it is only possible to focus the eyes on one plane in space at one time. Remembered seeing is usually a *series* of visual impressions.	A picture is limited entirely to the format, with the idea of space artificially achieved. Rhythmic lines and directions are sometimes used to unify a picture, and prevent it from appearing only as a fragment of nature.
Space and Volume	*Space and Volume*
Actual volume is seen in space with our two eyes, a "seeing around." This gives a sense of "roundness" of volumes. The sense of space and distance relationships in nature is aided by this fact, as well as by the memory of former experience in having traveled a similar distance in space before.	Space in pictures is purely an idea, existing as it does on a flat plane. Space differences here are seen simultaneously, without need to change the focus of the eyes. Space is created by overlapping, perspective, etc., volume by the use of light and shade, or by arbitrary shading in following form.

Light and Color Range

In the actual world, light and color are almost unlimited. The differences range from the lightest color in full sunlight to the darkest color in complete darkness.

Light and Color Range

Pictures employ artificial color and value relations to approximate the light and color of actuality. For instance, a very light color placed against a very dark one is necessary to produce a contrast similar to that in nature.

This arbitrary scale approximates the range of light and color in the actual world, as compared to the limited possibilities of pigment used in pictures.

Light and Color Range, Actual World

Light and Color Range,
Pigment

BEGINNING A
COMPOSITION

FIRST, ESTABLISH THE FORMAT

Ways of Beginning a Composition

There are perhaps as many ways of beginning a picture as there are painters to paint them, and individual painters will usually vary their methods as different problems arise. The only rule is to *trust your instincts,* for the actual beginning of a composition may have been far back in time, a small but remembered impression that must be finally realized in paint.

The following outline suggests only a few of the ways some painters begin.

Composing Directly from Nature

This approach, while not always the most creative, is perhaps the commonest method of beginning a composition. In painting directly from nature, it is always possible to find significant lines and directions

[36]

in the actual motif. It then becomes a matter of selection in eliminating nonessential elements from the material at hand. In this, or almost any approach to pictorial composition, it is desirable to keep the picture balanced at all stages, with the same degree of completion evenly distributed at all times.

Many painters also compose from *sketches* made from nature, combining several sketches in one picture, while others *partially* complete a picture out of doors, to be carried further in the studio.

Small Experimental Sketches

It is much simpler to visualize total effects in small areas than in large. A small sketch, not being large enough to allow accurate drawing, will necessarily depend for effects on its dark and light pattern. This pattern can then be enlarged and the final drawing adjusted to it.

Progressive Tracings

Tracing one experimental drawing from another until a composition is realized is often done, but it is desirable not to draw accurately too soon. For when the drawing is carried to completion before the composition is fully realized, it will be increasingly difficult to unify the two.

Linear Design First

Some painters begin with the linear design, a line drawing without dark or light pattern. When this linear design is satisfactory, the darks and lights are then experimentally placed on the previously established design.

Dynamic symmetry is primarily a linear system for arriving at proportions *on the flat picture plane,* and can be of little value in integrating two- and three-dimensional space.

Experimental Abstraction

Perhaps the most creative way to compose is to begin with abstract color shapes, shifting and transposing until a unified abstraction is fully realized. This can then be the final picture, pure abstraction without subject; or the abstract shapes may suggest subject matter which can be superimposed or integrated, but in such a way as *not to destroy the basic and already established abstract design.*

The Subject Is Not Important

Six miscellaneous objects are shown above, unrelated by subject, use, or literary associations. In other words, the objects in themselves do not "tell a story."

However, these objects have been selected for their variety of shape, for the bottle is fundamentally a cylinder, the jug a sphere, the ash tray a free and rhythmic form, while the three rectangles are purely geometric. As used in the following diagrams, these objects are considered only from this *abstract-without-subject* point of view, as a part of unified lines, shapes, and directions. But since almost all of the following diagrams emphasize *one* isolated aspect of pictorial composition, they will necessarily be incomplete as pictures.

Arrangement of Objects

In these two photographs, the six objects have been *arranged* by shifting the objects themselves, bringing them somewhat in accord with the dominant directions of their respective horizontal and vertical formats. We thus have two pictures of different proportions, which show the same six objects in two photographic arrangements.

Pictorial arrangement is the direct translation to a flat plane (by either drawing or photography) of forms, shapes, or objects in their *actual-world relationships*.

Arrangement of Objects Is Not Composition

If these two still-life "subjects" were to be translated into space composition where two-dimensional pattern is integrated with three-dimensional space, the *objects* themselves would then be drawn differently in their differing space relationships. As seen through the mind, the selective vision, and the personal feeling of an artist, their *shape* would be conditioned by their particular position in space, by their relation to their format and to surrounding objects, and by their two- and three-dimensional relation to the picture plane.

In this way, a composition can be completely unified where not one line, shape, or direction can be altered without destroying the entire picture.

This kind of pictorial composition, the integration of forms in space with personal feeling, is obviously impossible to duplicate by the camera's factual recording and unselective lens.

KINDS OF

COMPOSITION

Symmetrical Composition

Symmetry is perhaps the simplest form of pictorial composition (or arrangement) where a feeling of balance and stability is achieved by a centered vertical division of the format, each half of the picture reversing the other.

Symmetrical Composition

It is seldom that a picture is absolutely symmetrical, as in the diagram; for while this picture by Diego Rivera is predominately symmetrical, there is variety in the background shapes, the lilies, and the hair styles of the figures in the right and left foreground. Not only is the *drawing* symmetrical, but the dark and light value placing is evenly balanced as well.

DIEGO RIVERA: Flower Festival, Feast of Santa Anita. *Collection of the Museum of Modern Art, New York.*

Symmetrical Composition

This picture makes use of two white vertical lines supported by a white shape on a triangular dark base.

There is added variety in the curving light shape extending down from the right shoulder and across the arm to the table's edge and in the difference of the two extended hands.

Symmetrical Composition

William Blake has balanced the central figure by a supporting triangle, with variety in the rhythmic line directions throughout the picture.

Vertical Composition

There is nobility in a vertical line which can be experienced emotionally from its direction alone. Tall trees, tall buildings, or even tall people have a dignity in themselves from their dominant direction. A child attains the dignity of the vertical when he learns to walk upright.

A vertical line is positive; it follows the pull of gravity and helps to stabilize a composition by reaffirming two of the format lines.

Vertical Composition

The repeated verticals in this composition are interrupted at intervals by rhythmic horizontal directions.

FRANCISCO DOSAMANTES: Women of Oaxaca. *Collection of the Museum of Modern Art, New York.*

Vertical Composition

The strong vertical direction in this picture is dissipated at the upper edge by the horizontal effect of the hair, and in the lower section by the curving arms and hands. Thus, the general directions relate to the vertical format but are held *within* the picture by rhythmic curves and stabilizing horizontal lines.

WILLIAM DOBELL: The Strapper. *Photograph from British Information Services.*

Vertical Composition

Here dominant verticals unify angular shapes, lines, and directions in a highly disciplined abstract space composition.

Louis Guglielmi: Solitudes. *Courtesy of the Downtown Gallery.*

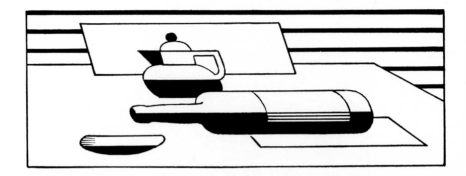

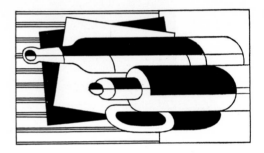

Horizontal Composition

A horizontal composition is very similar to a vertical *in a horizontal position*, both a reaffirmation of dominant format directions. The horizontal can be a line at rest, suggesting the passive, unbroken line of the horizon; or it can also represent a speed line which contradicts the quiet, restful feeling. Automobiles, speed boats, streamlined locomotives are all designed as horizontal forms to move in horizontal directions.

Horizontal Composition

While this is a horizontal composition, the spatial design is somewhat angular, a secondary movement leading into space with a return to the picture plane.

FRANK ALBERT MECHAU, JR.: Last of the Wild Horses. *Courtesy of the Metropolitan Museum of Art.*

Horizontal Composition

The centered division of light and dark adds to the horizontal feeling of this picture which also demonstrates the horizontal as a figurative speed line.

MORRIS GRAVES: Wounded Scoter. *The Cleveland Museum of Art.*

Horizontal Composition

The angular horizontal composition is held within the format by the tree forms at either end. Notice how a *subjective* vertical line is continued by the significant edge above the three dark windows.

LYONEL FEININGER: Three Windows. *Photograph courtesy of the Buchholz Gallery.*

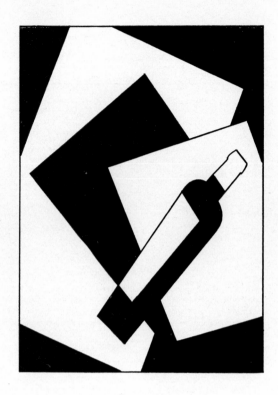

Angular Lines in Composition

Angular lines can be dynamic, off balance, unstable falling lines, or may also represent recession into pictorial space.

This diagram of angles, with no stabilizing horizontal or vertical lines, demonstrates dynamic movement in limited space. Certain effects in pictorial composition, where off-balanced lines are brought into balance by opposing directions, can be compared to the dance in its succession of balanced and off-balanced movements in both time and space.

Angular Lines in Composition

Movement in composition is, of course, not action in the sense of actual movement. Juan Gris has indicated rhythmic movement in this still life where no actual movement could be expected to occur. Horizontal and vertical lines help to stabilize this otherwise angular composition, while diagonals not only express rhythmic movements but also describe pictorial space.

JUAN GRIS: The Chessboard. *Collection of the Museum of Modern Art, New York.*

Angular Lines in Composition

This picture combines the effect of action *and pictorial movement.* The strong diagonal from lower left to upper right (a falling line) is opposed by a variety of curves and angles from the opposite direction.

JOSÉ CLEMENTE OROZCO: Barricade. *Collection of the Museum of Modern Art, New York.*

Angular Lines in Composition

In Rembrandt's *Storm on the Sea of Galilee*, it is the angular directions that contribute both to the movement in the picture and to the representational effect of the storm at sea. At the top of the mast many converging lines form a strong visual direction, counteracted and held within the picture by a rhythmic flowing line.

REMBRANDT VAN RYN: Storm on the Sea of Galilee. *Isabella Stewart Gardner Museum, Boston, Mass.*

Triangles in Composition

The equilateral triangle on a horizontal base is one of the most stable forms of composition (as it is in architecture), where each side of the triangle supports the other. But the triangle offers many other possibilities.

In this example by Joseph Hirsch, rather than indicating stability, two triangles unify the otherwise divided horizontal movement in a dominant horizontal direction.

JOSEPH HIRSCH: Two Men. *Collection of the Museum of Modern Art, New York.*

The Triangle in Composition

It is seldom that anyone *begins* a picture with the idea of incorporating triangles or similar geometric forms; it is only after the picture assumes some basic geometric pattern that corresponding geometric forms are finally integrated.

William Gropper has made an unusual use of the triangle in this picture, dynamic rather than stable, in unifying the subject with the angular construction of the picture.

WILLIAM GROPPER: Cavalry. *Photograph courtesy Associated American Artists.*

The Diagonal in Composition

The strong diagonal direction from lower left to upper right in this composition is balanced by many small opposing diagonal lines.

Opposed Diagonals in Composition

One diagonal is usually a falling line (if it does not describe space), but two opposing diagonals will support one another, balanced in equilibrium on the picture plane as in the above picture.

MARIE LAURENCIN: In the Park. *The Art Institute of Chicago.*

Rhythmic Line in Composition

A rhythmic line *moves,* is opulent, is unifying. The movement in the above diagram is centrifugal in direction, uniting the elements of the diagram into one rhythmic whole.

Rhythmic Line in Composition

The strong elliptical movement in Rubens' *The Peasant Dance* is also centrifugal in effect. The picture is stabilized, however, by the accented horizontal directions formed by the extended arms of the dancing figures.

PETER PAUL RUBENS: The Peasant Dance. *Prado, Madrid.*

Rhythmic Line in Composition

It cannot be repeated too often that one of the qualities of space composition is the possibility of seeing the picture both flat and deep at the same time.

In Jean Charlot's lithograph, rhythmic lines unite both background and foreground planes, particularly in the line which descends from the upper-right background, continuing down the outside of the child's arm to be turned up again by the curving fold at the lower edge of the child's dress.

JEAN CHARLOT: Mother and Child. *Collection of the Museum of Modern Art, New York.*

Rhythmic Line in Composition

William Palmer has rhythmically integrated the foreground and background of this picture by implied or subjective lines that visually unite the upturned ski directions with the curving lines in the background hills. This effect is spatially similar to the rhythmic integration in Charlot's *Mother and Child*.

WILLIAM PALMER: Snow Ridge, Turin. *Photograph courtesy of the Midtown Galleries.*

The Self-Contained Picture

A self-contained picture is complete within itself, not being confined in any particular format.

The picture shown above is painted on the walls of a church and is self-contained in the area it occupies. But even so, the horizontal-vertical-angular-rhythmic relationships function very much as though the picture were designed for a specific format.

HANS FEIBUSCH: Mural. *Methodist Church, Colliers Wood, England.*

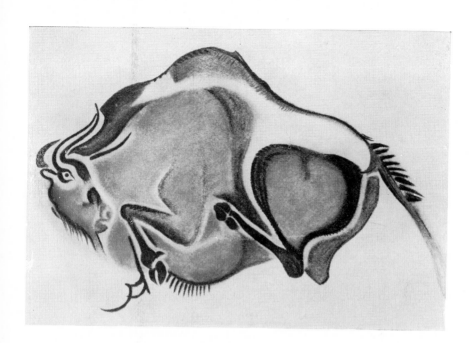

The Self-Contained Picture

Perhaps the cave man who painted this bison did not consciously design the picture to be self-contained, but the smaller linear rhythms are nevertheless integrated into the self-contained rhythmic movement of the whole.

Cave Painting, Altamira, Spain. *Photograph courtesy the American Museum of Natural History.*

SOME TECHNICAL

QUALITIES

Texture

There are many ways to use texture in painting, the above diagram illustrating only the application of a consistent texture over the entire surface, which helps to flatten a picture in relation to the picture plane. This is contrary (and preferable) to the "hole in the wall" type of representational painting, where a rough texture in the foreground is "smoothed out" as forms in the picture recede, creating an *illusion* of distance, a hole, rather than the effect of limited pictorial space.

Texture

To further accent the foregoing discussion of consistent texture, imagine this van Gogh landscape having a sky without texture of any kind.

VINCENT VAN GOGH: Cypresses by Moonlight. *Courtesy of Oxford University Press, New York, and Phaidon Press, Vienna.*

Texture

On this page from an early Chinese drawing book, leaves are shown *first* as textures and only secondarily as parts of trees.

Szu Dzu-Huän: Landscape Drawing Book, Ming Dynasty. *From the collection of Howard Willard.*

[74]

Texture

This composition by Paul Klee contrasts directional planes of texture with nontextured areas in varying positions in space.

PAUL KLEE: Strawberry Inn. *Photograph courtesy of J. B. Neumann.*

Outline

An outline of even width (not decreasing in size as it appears to recede in space) will still indicate recession but without destroying the flatness of the picture plane.

Outline

This landscape by De Hirsh Margules is similar to the diagram in that the outline is part both of the pictorial space and of the pattern *on* the picture plane.

DE HIRSH MARGULES: Portuguese Dock, Gloucester. *Collection of the Museum of Modern Art, New York.*

Outline

In Roualt's *St. Veronica* (designed for a stained-glass window), the outline becomes a pattern on *one* spatial plane, having the same flattening effect as the leaded line in any stained-glass window.

GEORGES ROUAULT: St. Veronica. *Photograph courtesy of the Information Division, French Embassy.*

[78]

Outline

This is a free use of outline where a superimposed line is independent of other shapes in the composition, a freedom allowing two different conceptions to be combined on the same area at the same time.

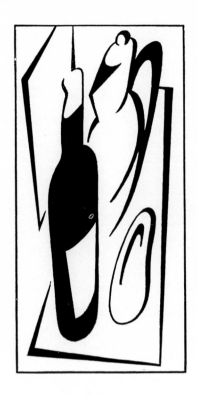

Subjective Lines

This diagram demonstrates (among other ideas) *subjective lines,* where a *felt* direction is implied, to be visually completed by the observer of the picture.

The spout of the jug in the diagram, as an example, optically connects with the upper black edge of the bottle as a *subjective line,* and the upper part of the bottle's label continues into the curving line around the lower part of the jug in a similar way.

Subjective Lines

E. McKnight Kauffer has created subjective lines in this poster which not only contribute to the dynamic movement but also become part of both pattern and space.

E. McKnight Kauffer: The Early Bird (poster). *Collection of the Museum of Modern Art, New York.*

Subjective Lines

A *subjective line* may also consist of many smaller directions which combine to form one dominant but implied directional line.

Subjective Lines

In this painting by Paul Gauguin, a vertical subjective line starts from the post in the upper right and continues down through the figure to the foot, ending in the fruit at the bottom edge of the picture.

PAUL GAUGUIN: Seated Woman. *Courtesy of the Worcester Art Museum.*

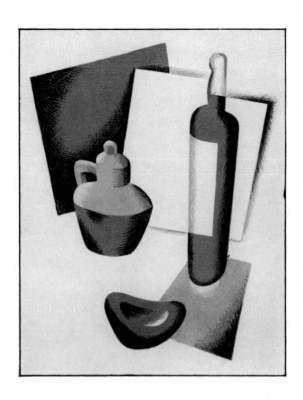

Significant Edges

Significant edges are graduated accents, a strong dark contrasted against a light value or vice versa, not as an indication of light and shade but as a purely arbitrary accent.

Significant edges are one way to compensate for the limitations of pigment in representing contrasts as compared to the much greater range of a light and dark in the actual world.

Significant Edges

Significant edges can also accent recession of spatial planes, as in this picture by Paul Klee where accented planes overlap from lower right to upper left in space.

PAUL KLEE: Meeting Place in Winter. *Photograph courtesy of J. B. Neumann.*

[85]

Significant Edges

Significant edges create a textural effect over most of this picture's surface and, in addition, accent vertical, horizontal, and diagonal lines. And while some spatial recession is indicated in this composition, the many small significant edges unite to form a flat pattern closely related to the picture plane.

JUAN GRIS: Guitar and Flowers. *Collection of the Museum of Modern Art, New York.*

Significant Edges

The significant edges in this El Greco accent such directions as the diagonal drapery in the lower right, the pillar and arch in the middle distance, and many other secondary movements throughout the picture.

EL GRECO· The Adoration of the Shepherds. *Courtesy of the Metropolitan Museum of Art.*

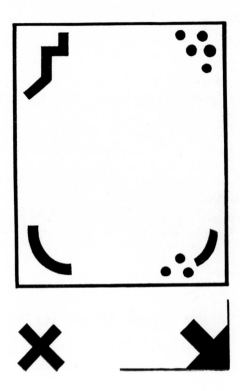

Corners Are Arrows

The right angles formed by the corners of any picture are natural arrows; and any form, line, or direction, as it approaches a corner, becomes increasingly important in a composition. Not only do corners create visual arrows, but lines which cross at right angles, unless otherwise compensated for, will produce focal points which may interfere with the flow of rhythmic organization.

Corners Are Arrows

The simplified diagram on the opposite page illustrates how Paul Gauguin solved the corner problems in this picture, movement being carried *around* each corner by a different abstract means.

PAUL GAUGUIN: Seated Woman. *Courtesy of the Worcester Art Museum.*

SOME DO'S
AND DON'T'S

Funnel-Effect Pictures

The funnel effect in pictures is partially brought about by the concentration of attention at a focal point in the distance, a static center of interest, which stops all rhythmic movement by a recession into space without return. This results in a "hole in the wall" effect caused by destroying the integrity (flatness) of the picture plane.

Funnel-Effect Pictures

In this funnel-effect picture, attention is directed to the *darkest* dark value (the two figures) against the *lightest* light; and since this same contrast is not repeated elsewhere, interest is held at that point with no opportunity for further visual exploration.

ARTIST UNKNOWN: Cathedral.

Avoiding a Funnel Effect

This picture also shows a recession into space, but the funnel effect is counteracted by the rhythmic movement leading into space and returning to the picture plane. The distant windows are not symmetrical, which would focus attention on them, but are rhythmically related to the larger forms moving throughout the picture.

ROBERT DELAUNEY: Saint Severin. *Minneapolis Institute of Arts.*

Avoiding a Funnel Effect

While this picture recedes somewhat in the manner of a funnel picture, interest is controlled by the interval directions in the *foreground* plane, an elliptical visual path through the near figures to the canopy above, with a return to the foreground plane.

HIERONYMUS BOSCH: Adoration of the Kings. *Courtesy of the Metropolitan Museum of Art.*

Aerial Perspective

Aerial perspective (an effect possible to see in nature) suggests distance by a progressive lightening of values, a fading out of forms as they recede. But an attempt to copy this illusion from nature will carry interest *back* into a picture and, like the funnel effect, will offer no opportunity for a return to the picture plane.

Aerial Perspective

This progressive stepping back of values may also concentrate what interest there is on the foreground and, like a carelessly taken photograph, leave empty and uninteresting areas in the remainder of the picture.

JOHN FREDERICK KENSETT: Lake George. *Courtesy of the Metropolitan Museum of Art.*

Filling the Format

Any part of a composition that doesn't work *for* the picture will work against it.

In El Greco's *View of Toledo,* no part of the picture is empty, but all is filled with vital, definite statements, all in accord with the subject, the format, and the picture plane.

EL GRECO: View of Toledo. *Courtesy of the Metropolitan Museum of Art.*

Filling the Format

While the figures and buildings in this picture appear *smaller* as they recede in space, they *do not* get correspondingly lighter in value through aerial perspective; instead, the *dark* shapes form a spatial pattern over the composition's entire area.

UNKNOWN FLEMISH PAINTER: Christ Bearing the Cross. *Courtesy of the Metropolitan Museum of Art.*

Uncontrolled Shadows

Shadows in nature usually (but not always) help to define form, but their literal transcription to a flat plane is apt to be confusing if the shadow's shape is not also considered as an abstract element in a picture's design.

Uncontrolled Shadows

The use of accidental shadows to destroy form is the foundation of certain types of camouflage, notably disruptive pattern, and is similar in effect to the confusion in the picture shown above.

JOHN SINGER SARGENT: The Hermit. *Courtesy of the Metropolitan Museum of Art.*

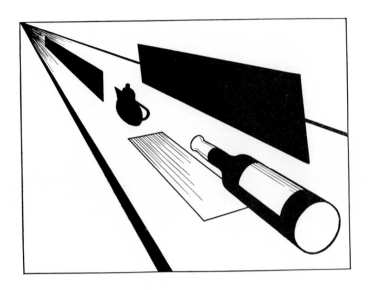

Too Much Perspective

Perspective is a mechanical and inflexible system where lines converge at vanishing points to give the illusion of distance. Once these vanishing points are established, however, the system takes over and forces the painter into channels not of his own choosing.

In the above diagram, the sharp convergence creates an arrowlike direction leading the eye completely *out of the picture.*

Too Much Perspective

This Currier and Ives lithograph is similar to the diagram in that converging lines direct attention *outside* the picture area.

CURRIER AND IVES: Across the Continent.

Overcoming the Faults of Perspective

When any directional thrust becomes too compelling, it may be modified without changing the drawing by a superimposed pattern as a counter movement of opposing directions.

Overcoming the Faults of Perspective

The bridge railing in Edvard Munch's picture creates a dominant thrust to the right, a direction which would have carried completely out of the right side but for the retarding effect of the vertical lines of the three girls on the bridge and the change in direction of the curved lines at the railings' extreme end.

EDVARD MUNCH: Three Girls on a Bridge. *National Gallery, Oslo, Norway.*

Protrusion from the Picture Plane

This effect is startling, a virtue, perhaps, in advertising; but since it is impossible to stay startled for long, this breaking of the picture plane is of dubious value in painting a picture of enduring worth.

In this diagram, the vertical edge of the table has been established *on* the picture plane by its right-hand junction with the table top. This plane being thus established, anything forward of this point will inevitably appear to protrude from the picture plane.

Protrusion from the Picture Plane

This picture is unusual in that *everything* protrudes, for nothing is *behind* the picture plane. If the picture were hung on a wall, the ball, tack, and string would appear to stand out from the wall itself and into the actual space of the room.

E. K. HAWLEY: Hanging Sphere. *Study Collection of the Museum of Modern Art, New York.*

Bumps and Hollows on the Picture Plane

To preserve the integrity of the picture plane is to keep the picture surface visually flat, without the illusion of protruding bumps or simulated hollows.

This picture, however, does create the illusion of bumps and hollows on an otherwise plane surface. The hat, hands, and lower part of the shirt appear to protrude, while the under side of the hat is obviously a hollow on the picture plane. Some reasons for this illusionary effect are the placing of forms in relation to the format and the lack of stabilizing and flattening horizontal and vertical lines.

DAVID ALFARO SIQUEIROS: Ethnography. *Collection of the Museum of Modern Art, New York.*

[108]

"Fooling the Eye"

Great painting never attempts to "fool you" into thinking it is not a painting but the thing itself, any more than great music reproduces only actual sounds in accidental relationships.

There is great technical skill shown in this example of what the French call *trompe l'oeil*, or "cheat the eye" painting, but it is still a deception and not the thing itself. Aside from its deceptive quality, parts of this picture protrude from the picture plane.

PIERRE ROY: Daylight Saving Time. *Collection of the Museum of Modern Art, New York.*

SURREALISM

AND

ABSTRACTION

Surrealism

Max Ernst, in an article, *Inspiration to Order* [*Art of This Century*, Peggy Guggenheim, New York, 1942], gives as one of the principles of surrealism "the pairing of two realities which apparently cannot be paired on a plane apparently not suited to them"—or, to simplify, things in associations not usually found in the actual world.

With this in mind, let us examine Salvador Dali's *The Persistence of Memory* where rigid watches are made to bend. Here are the two dissimilar associations, watches *don't* bend, watches *do* bend. But if the observer is unaware that watches are fundamentally rigid, the expected shock is unlikely to occur. Thus the subject is foremost and the viewpoint is literary—the result is illustrative perhaps, but has little in common with the visual possibilities in painting.

SALVADOR DALI: The Persistence of Memory. *Collection of the Museum of Modern Art, New York.*

Surrealism

Pieter Huys was a sixteenth-century "surrealist" in his pairing of dissimilar objects and associations. In this picture he has painted a fish in the sky, animal heads on human bodies, combined unnatural size relationships, and many other "realities which apparently cannot be paired" in their actual-world relationships.

Surrealism is also a reversal of the principle behind magazine-cover pictures, where things previously associated are reassembled to tell a story in pictures that might also be told in words, both depending on the observer's previous knowledge of the objects shown.

PIETER HUYS: The Temptation of St. Anthony. *Courtesy of the Metropolitan Museum of Art.*

Abstraction

Every organized picture is an abstraction to some extent in the use of abstract (without subject) shapes for unifying the composition.

Although this picture has a human-interest subject, its abstract construction is based on a series of related rectangles in varying positions in space.

PIETER DE HOOCH: The Visit. *Courtesy of the Metropolitan Museum of Art.*

Abstraction

This is a "pure abstraction," a flat pattern without pictorial space; and while it has no recognizable subject, its rectangular organization is very similar to the painting by Pieter de Hooch on the opposite page.

Abstraction

Like the preceding Mondrian picture, this "pure abstraction" has no recognizable subject; but unlike the Mondrian, this composition integrates both pattern *and pictorial space*. In these three pictures, Mondrian has used pattern only, Charles Howard has used pattern *and* space, while Pieter de Hooch combined a *subject* with both pattern and pictorial space.

CHARLES HOWARD: Composition. *Courtesy of the Nierendorf Gallery.*

Degree of Abstraction

On the following two facing pages is an "abstraction chart" from my earlier book, *Pictures, Painters, and You*, and is included here to show varying degrees of abstraction in composing pictures. The word *abstraction* as used here, means degree *away* from nature and not abstracted from it. Hence, the chart begins with the accidental realism of the subject, a church (not used in the chart as a photograph, but as representing the church itself), then through increasing degrees of abstraction to a complete lack of subject, to abstraction in its purest form. Please bear in mind that these pictures are diagrams, not works of art, and are used merely to help clarify an idea.

It will be found that most pictures can be compared in degree of abstraction to some position on this chart; and while varying degrees of abstraction are shown, they are all arbitrary and could have been shown in any number of different ways.

Pure abstraction logically belongs at the extreme end of the chart, but it is somewhat different from the others as it is usually conceived without reference to objects in the actual world. And while the chart shows progressive abstraction, it is intended to show a direction only, rather than to indicate one degree as being better than another. To be of value, this chart should be interpreted only in a broad and general way.

1. *Subject;* complete emphasis on subject without personal point of view. Forms and spaces, light and shade, all in the accidental relationships of the actual world.

2. *Subject simplified,* but forms and spaces, light and shade still pictorially unrelated. A collection of useful facts, but otherwise pictorially uninteresting.

5. *More abstract* than the preceding, it is essentially the same in drawing, but elements have been simplified; the pattern overlaying picture has changed.

6. *Transparency;* pattern and space are more evident as church parallels picture plane, triangular space pattern penetrates through church. Based on horizontal, vertical, diagonal.

3. *Arranged,* to some extent, by centering the church, shifting trees and placing clouds in the sky, figure added for human interest. An illustrative picture.

4. *Unified* to the picture's format, with a scheme of opposing diagonals to organize forms, to bring the church, road, hills, trees, and figures into closer pictorial relationship.

7. *Near abstraction,* still has pattern and space, but subject almost entirely disappears, due to removal of descriptive steeple, windows and figures.

8. *Pure abstraction,* without space or subject. Pure abstraction would not necessarily be developed in the foregoing steps, but could be composed without reference to the actual world.

[119]

1. *Photograph of the motif.* Here are the three rectangles which originally suggested the final painting. This series first appeared in *The Studio*, London.

RAY BETHERS

2. *Sketch from nature.* This was the first step among several later compositional sketches which led up to the painting opposite.

3. *The final painting* (*by* Ray Bethers). Compare this completed composition with the diagram of abstract shapes shown below.

4. *Abstract elements in the painting.* The dark shapes in this diagram are emphasized to show their abstract relationships.

Two Broad Divisions of Pictures (Closed)

Almost any composition will fall into one or the other of two divisions of pictures. In "closed" compositions, the light and dark areas are confined within their own boundaries. But in "open" composition, the light and dark patterns are purely arbitrary and not confined to the boundaries of forms.

The above diagram illustrates "closed" composition, where the light and dark areas are confined to the shapes of objects.

Two Broad Divisions of Pictures (Closed)

This closed composition also has limited light and shade, which is used to describe individual forms rather than to make arbitrary shapes in the total composition.

FRANCESCO PESELLINO: The Crucifixion with St. Jerome and St. Francis. *National Gallery of Art, Washington, D.C. (Kress Collection).*

Two Broad Divisions of Pictures (Closed)

This closed picture by an unknown folk painter is composed of three simple values, with the secondary forms and textures within each value subordinated to the larger shapes and held within their boundaries.

ARTIST UNKNOWN: Cat. *Found in New Hampshire about 1845. Courtesy of the Harry Stone Gallery.*

Two Broad Divisions of Pictures (Closed)

The dark (and confined) shapes in the foreground of this picture combine with the dark background shapes in both two- and three-dimensional design.

BEN SHAHN: Italian Landscape I. *Walker Art Center.*

Two Broad Divisions of Pictures (Open)

In "open" composition, as outlined before, the light and dark patterns are arbitrary and are not confined to the boundaries of forms. This is demonstrated in the two diagrams above, dissimilar in style but both having arbitrary light and dark areas which, in themselves, dominate any light and dark patterns derived from individual forms.

Two Broad Divisions of Pictures (Open) The "Passage"

One way to prevent single objects from becoming "closed," and thus stand out individually, is to create *passages* from one to another.

A *"passage"* is a point where *one* color becomes part of *two* objects. This allows the eye to pass easily from one object to another, without being held within any one self-contained contour.

In the above diagram I have made a *passage* from the light foreground, which continues through each succeeding object to the darkest area in the upper right background.

There is also a certain element of mystery where contours are missing, and must then be imaginatively supplied.

Two Broad Divisions of Pictures (Open)

In Rembrandt's *Christ Healing the Sick*, the composition is divided into two arbitrary areas, light and dark, with the figures in each subordinated (and contained) inside the value of their particular plane. In other words, the planes are not dependent on the shapes of the objects within them.

This conception of open composition is similar to the left-hand diagram on page 126.

REMBRANDT VAN RYN: Christ Healing the Sick.

Two Broad Divisions of Pictures (Open)

At first glance one would not think that Dufy and Rembrandt had much in common, and yet they have, for both use arbitrary planes which do not correspond to the shapes or objects within them. For instance, the rectangular light plane in the lower right of the above picture dominates the superimposed line drawing, just as Rembrandt's larger planes dominate his figures. Dufy's style is best represented by the right-hand diagram on page 126, where the boundaries of all planes are more clearly defined.

RAOUL DUFY: La Dogana. *Photograph by courtesy of the Bignon Gallery.*

NEW SHAPES

FROM OLD

Making New Shapes from Old

The diagram on the left is a simple *arrangement* of two isolated objects.

The other diagram, however, illustrates a basic principle of pictorial composition where a new *and unifying* shape common to both objects is created, a shape which did not exist before. This possibility allows great freedom in composing, a freedom from the actual shapes of things, and in addition contributes to the "self-renewing" quality of pictures.

Making New Shapes from Old

The geometric light area in the background of this picture takes on added meaning from the new shape created by its combination with the two figures on the foreground plane. This permits the far and near planes to be seen either as one, or as two in their spatial relationship.

José Clemente Orozco: Peace. *Collection of the Museum of Modern Art. New York.*

Making New Shapes from Old

The larger light and dark areas in this picture are somewhat arbitrary, and are not entirely dictated by the contours of individual forms. This is best shown by the dark robe of the central figure, which becomes part of a larger dark and rhythmic shape, while the feet and lower part of the figure belong to the lighter area of the composition.

Duccio: Temptation of Christ. *Copyright, the Frick Collection, New York.*

Making New Shapes from Old

Here a great many shapes grow into and become part of other shapes. The plate in the foreground, for instance, is also part of 'the free form which expands into the sheet of music and over most of the front part of the table, and is then carried into the outline of the mandolin and the shape directly behind.

Georges Braque: The Table. *Courtesy of the Art Institute of Chicago.*

[135]

New Shapes from Old (Contained)

The larger areas of this picture have been divided into smaller confined shapes, with each shape not only a contained composition in itself,
but also integrated into the composition as a whole.

TINTORETTO: The Worship of the Golden Calf. *National Gallery of Art, Washington,*
D.C. (*Kress Collection*).

New Shapes from Old (Contained)

This picture illustrates *one* contained shape; the outer contour of the madonna is hardly evident in contrast to the unity of the larger rhythmic unit of light values against the dark background.

MORETTI: Madonna and Child. *Courtesy of the Metropolitan Museum of Art.*

New Shapes from Old (Distortion)

The accurate transcription of any symmetrical form (one side repeating the other) is apt to appear static and isolated from other forms in composing a picture.

The above diagram, adapted from Cézanne's *Still Life with Apples and Oranges*, shows this isolation. In the diagram, the three still-life objects have been made symmetrical in contrast to the integrating distortion introduced by Cézanne in the picture on the opposite page.

New Shapes from Old (Distortion)

The shape of objects in this space composition is conditioned by their relative position in pictorial space, for each would have been drawn differently if transferred to another spatial position.

PAUL CÉZANNE: Still Life with Apples and Oranges. *Louvre, Paris.*

New Shapes from Old (without Distortion)

It is possible to integrate symmetrical objects in a composition without distortion by superimposing patterns of dark and light which dominate the symmetry of the actual forms, as in the above diagram.

New Shapes from Old

While this picture does not exactly parallel the diagram, it does show various methods of integrating symmetrical forms into a composition. The dark circle in the lower center, for instance, is a segment only, the two sides of the bottle are treated differently, and the fruit bowl is not symmetrically drawn.

JUAN GRIS: Grapes and Wine. *Collection of the Museum of Modern Art, New York.*

Arbitrary Proportions

The conception of arbitrary proportions allows forms to be relatively enlarged or made smaller for either psychological or design reasons. In this composition, the psychological importance of the Virgin establishes the relative sizes of all the figures in the picture. The design of the picture springs from this arbitrary relation.

GIOVANNI BARONZIO: The Adoration of the Magi. *National Gallery of Art, Washington, D.C. (Kress Collection).*

Arbitrary Proportions

Relative sizes in this picture are established by design, for the largest figure in the composition (important only in size) is in the *background*, while the smallest figure is on the *foreground* plane.

JACOB LAWRENCE: One of the Largest Race Riots Occurred in East St. Louis. *Collection of the Museum of Modern Art, New York.*

UNIFYING

A COMPOSITION

Unifying Darks for Integration

This is perhaps the most important section in the book, for when any composition shows weakness, it is usually in the organization of *darks* in the compositional design.

In the above diagram, darks describe form, indicate near and far space, and are collectively a rhythmic pattern *on* the picture plane.

The dark organization can be the underlying structure which allows "first things first" to be seen, a simulation of time where there is no time.

Unifying Darks for Integration

The variety of dark shapes in this picture form a flat pattern, describe form, and thrust into space with a return to the picture plane. Try to think of this composition in terms of pattern only, next as pictorial space, and finally as both in combination. Turn the picture upside down, if necessary, to see it as an abstract design of dark shapes without subject connotations.

WARD LOCKWOOD: Midwinter. *Permanent Collection, Addison Gallery of Art, Andover, Mass.*

Unifying Darks for Integration

This diagram is a simplification of the dark design in Pieter Breughel's *Huntsmen in the Snow*, where an elliptical spatial movement is combined with two opposed diagonals and the stabilizing effect of horizontal and vertical lines.

Unifying Darks for Integration

While this is a discussion of *darks* in organizing pictures, dark does not mean black, but any dark value of any color.

PIETER BREUGHEL: The Huntsmen in the Snow. *Vienna Museum.*

Unifying Darks for Integration (Interval)

Interval is the sum total of the various shapes (usually, but not always, dark in value) which direct interest through, on, and around a picture.

JOHN MARIN: Camden Mountain across the Bay. *Collection of the Museum of Modern Art, New York.*

[150]

Unifying Darks for Integration (Interval)

Braque combines textures with inventive dark shapes in the interval of this picture.

GEORGES BRAQUE: Nature Morte—Fond Rose. *Courtesy of the Rosenberg Galleries.*

[151]

Unifying Lights for Integration

This diagram is *not* a reversal of values from the preceding diagram of darks, although the linear design is the same.

Integrating a composition by *light* values, however, is very similar to the use of darks, it being the particular interval of shapes and directions of light or dark that usually helps to unify any picture.

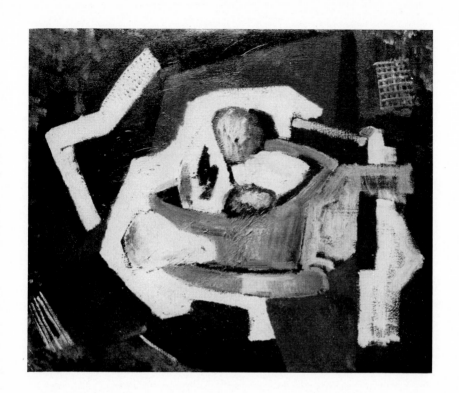

Unifying Lights for Integration

It is the *light* shapes and directions in this still life that unite the dark and middle values in a combined pattern and space organization.

MARSDEN HARTLEY: Still Life with Fruit. *From the private collection of Bertha Schaefer.*

THE COMBINATION OF

PATTERN WITH

PICTORIAL SPACE

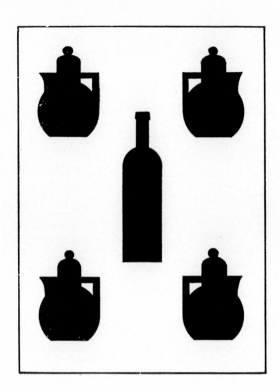

Pattern without Space

This diagram is a simple repeat pattern, geometric and without space. It is decorative in the same sense that pattern on fabric is decorative, where it creates no illusion of space and does not destroy the flatness of the surface on which it appears. This flat quality permits an almost unlimited use of pattern in the applied arts, where the emotional qualities which can result from the combination of pattern with pictorial space are not always to be desired.

Pattern without Space

This is a decorative pattern picture, not entirely flat, but still with definitely limited space.

Mario Carreño: The Bathers. *Photograph courtesy of the Perls Galleries.*

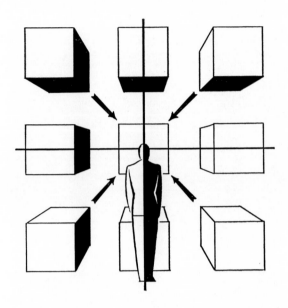

Space from a Fixed Vantage Point

There are many conceptions of pictorial space, not all in accord with one another; but space from a fixed vantage point is perhaps the clearest method of indicating space on a flat plane.

In the above diagram, space is divided into four sections, each in relation to the fixed position of the observer, the arrow in each division pointing *back* in space. Any one, two, or four of these divisions can be used in a rectangular format, but the clearest description of space will be found in either of the two lower sections where space is seen from above *and recedes in one direction only.* The strong spatial thrust in any of these single divisions, however, may carry interest *out* of a picture unless counteracted by other compositional means.

V

>   <

Λ

Space from a Fixed Vantage Point

This picture is composed of all four divisions of space. By placing the
edges of two sheets of paper to coincide with the four division points,
the various space divisions can be seen; and where these horizontal and
vertical lines cross is the observer's fixed vantage point.

MASTER OF THE BARBERINI PANELS: The Annunciation. *National Gallery of Art,
Washington, D.C.* (*Kress Collection*).

Space from Multiple Vantage Points

This diagram shows space seen from *two* vantage points, from the front and from directly above at the same time. This idea has been called a space-time concept, but there can be no actual time in the immobility of the picture surface.

Space from Multiple Vantage Points

This composition, from the standpoint of the same two vantage points, is identical with the diagram on the opposite page, with limited spatial recession in both the diagram and picture.

Fred Meyer: Sea Food and Red Wine. *Photograph courtesy of the Midtown Galleries.*

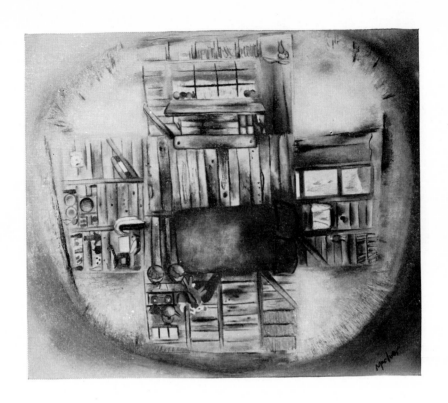

Space from Multiple Vantage Points

Here *five* simultaneous vantage points not only flatten the picture, but allow great freedom in expressing more than the eye can possibly see.

Loren MacIver: Shack. *Collection of the Museum of Modern Art, New York.*

Space from Multiple Periods of Time

This Futurist painting differs from the others in this section in that it attempts to show space from a fixed point of view *over a period of time*. This conception is set forth in the *Manifesto of the Futurist Painters, 1910*, as follows:

"In fact, all things move and run, all things change rapidly. The profile before our eyes is never static but constantly appears and disappears. Given the persistence of the image in the retina, moving objects are multiplied, changing their shapes as they pursue one another like lively vibrations across space."

GIACOMO BALLA: Dog on Leash. *Collection of A. Conger Goodyear; photograph courtesy of the Museum of Modern Art, New York.*

[163]

Space from Multiple Vantage Points

The head in profile with eyes seen from the front is another illustration of two simultaneous vantage points in space.

PABLO PICASSO: Seated Woman. *Collection of Mr. and Mrs. Lee A. Ault.*

Space from Multiple Vantage Points

Thirteen hundred years before Christ, the Egyptians were using multiple vantage points to present the human figure in its most significant aspects, where the eyes and torso are seen from the front, with the head, arms, and legs in profile.

EGYPTIAN, ABOUT 1300 B.C. (*Detail*). From *The Art of Ancient Egypt—Phaidon Press, Vienna, and Oxford University Press, New York.*

Space by Overlapping Planes

The diagram on the left shows overlapping planes as they recede in space irrespective of their size and contrary to the laws of perspective.

In their relation to the picture plane, the first three planes on the left are static and parallel to the picture plane; the next is tilted back, followed by a plane both tilted and turned while the four planes on the right are thrusting planes.

The landscape diagram describes space by planes which overlap both from near to far and far to near.

Confused Pictorial Space

Space in this picture moves from lower right to upper left, which establishes the dog in the frontal plane. Next in space is the angel (fixed by the position of the feet), but the figure of the boy *overlaps* the angel which would then place him in *front* of the angel and unsupported in space. Yet the right hand of the man (far back in space) performs the impossible by touching the head of the boy in forward, but unestablished space.

ANGELO PUCCINELLI: Tobit Blessing His Son. *National Gallery of Art, Washington, D.C. (Kress Collection).*

Overlapping Planes in Space

As abstract as this picture appears to be, the spatial planes still overlap in a recession similar to space in the actual world.

Planes from 1 to 12, resting on plane A in progressive recession, are all static and parallel to the picture plane except the dynamic planes 9 and 10, which indicate other directions. Plane X, however, is transparent and suspended in unestablished space.

Overlapping Planes in Space

While the planes in this picture are in varying positions in space, the patterns and textures on the individual planes also help to establish their particular spatial directions.

Mario Carreño: The Promenade. *Photograph courtesy of the Perls Galleries.*

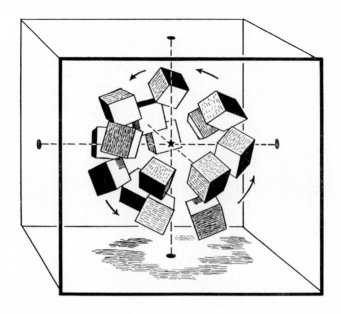

Rotating Volumes in Space

This diagram represents *an approach to thinking* rather than *a method for the actual representation of volumes* in pictorial space. In this concept, volumes rotate about a central point in cubic space *behind* the picture plane, unified somewhat in the manner of a small planetary system.

Rotating Volumes in Space

With the opposite diagram in mind, try to visualize a central point in this landscape in its relation to the volumes which "revolve" about this mythical central point.

PAUL CÉZANNE: Landscape with Viaduct. *Courtesy of the Metropolitan Museum of Art.*

Rotating Volumes in Space

The spatial design in this diagram, simplified from the painting on the opposite page, is somewhat elliptical, thrusting back in space with a consequent return to the picture plane.

Rotating Volumes in Space

The thrusting spatial directions are far more subtle in the picture itself, where movement is created by the interval of the figures, the relationship of the boxes on the right, and the curving and staccato patterns in the bridge and background buildings.

NICOLAI CIKOVSKY: River Front in St. Louis. *Collection of the Pepsi-Cola Company.*

Rotating Volumes in Space

This is a simplified diagram of the Poussin painting opposite, the star indicating the axis of the volumes "moving" around this spatial point.

Rotating Volumes in Space

Another way to *think* of this rotating-volume concept is to visualize the central point as the hub of a spherical "wheel," with the spokes extending in *all* directions.

Vertical Space Organization

While other pictorial ideas are contained in this diagram, it is included here to specifically demonstrate vertical space, to show the spatial relationship between the dark plane on the lower foreground to the *under* side of the table directly above.

Vertical Space Organization

While vertical space has been emphasized, it cannot be considered alone, but only as a *part* of space *behind* the picture plane.

K. Vialov: Ping Pong. *Collection of J. B. Neumann.*

Space by Tension

This diagram shows the "pull" or tension which may be set up between planes or forms by their particular shape and placing in pictorial space.

The implied triangle extending into space in the above diagram illustrates tension by subjective lines.

Space by Tension

There is an implied spatial triangle between the two foreground figures and the number high up on the background wall, while other tensions are set up by the dark staccato interval of figures and buildings in various planes of space.

BEN SHAHN: Handball. *Collection of the Museum of Modern Art, New York.*

NICOLAS POUSSIN: Moses Defending the Daughters of Jethro from the Insolent Shepherds. *Minneapolis Institute of Arts.*

Poussin's Use of Space

The framework of this composition has been separated into four parts, each linear diagram illustrating only *one* idea from the picture as a whole.

Triangles extend into space but are also pattern on the picture plane.

[180]

Verticals stabilize, repeat lines of the format, flatten the picture.

Horizontals also stabilize, and unify as dominant lines in the composition.

Rhythmic lines flow from background to foreground, giving movement.

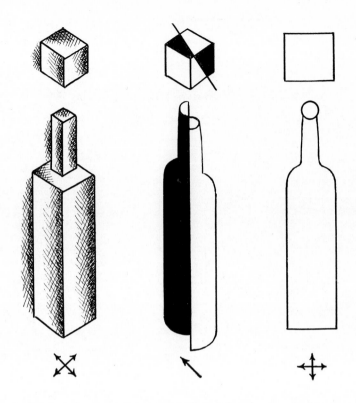

Three Space Conceptions of Cubism

In a broad way, Cubism can be divided into three clearly marked phases, one stemming from the other over a period of time.

I. (Left diagram) Cubism began with the principle of creating cubic volumes in pictorial space. These volumes, however, had a tendency to protrude from the picture plane.

II. (Center diagram) In the second phase, lines were superimposed *over* the volumes, or forms were represented by segments in an effort to control the tendency of volumes to protrude.

III. (Right diagram) In the third step, three-dimensional volume was replaced by two-dimensional shape.

Three Space Conceptions of Cubism—I

Here are solid, cubic volumes in space, with reversed perspective in the foreground to prevent protrusion from the picture plane.

PABLO PICASSO: Village in Tarragona. *Present owner unknown.*

Three Space Conceptions of Cubism—II

The volume in this bottle does not protrude, for first of all, it is incomplete, a segment; and second, it is flattened at the base by a superimposed horizontal line. The white lines of the violin also have a flattening effect, as do the many other vertical and horizontal lines.

JUAN GRIS: Violin and Engraving. *Collection of the Museum of Modern Art, New York.*

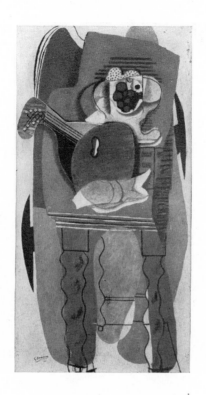

Three Space Conceptions of Cubism—III

Here three-dimensional volume has been replaced by two-dimensional shapes seen either from the front or from directly above. By this use of multiple vantage points, spatial recession can still be indicated but is limited by the resulting compression of pictorial space.

GEORGES BRAQUE: Le Buffet. *Collection of Mr. and Mrs. Jacques Helft.*

Shifting Planes in Space (Cubist)

Implied directions between shifting planes in space can develop a rhythm which almost appears to move both in space and time.

Shifting Planes in Space (Japanese)

The shifting planes in Cubism were usually arbitrary, but planes descriptive of actual forms (as in the above print) will function in a similar way in like relationships.

Tori Kiyotada (1715). Print (detail). *From Japanese Prints of the Primitive Period in the Collection of Louis V. Ledoux; E. Weyhe, New York, 1942.*

Various Attitudes toward Pictorial Space

These paintings are part of a set of twenty-five, all painted by the author for use in teaching.

1. *Photograph of the motif.* All of the diagrammatic paintings shown here derive from this subject.

2. *Manner of Cézanne.* Cézanne created space through the recessive quality of cold color and the advancing effect of warm.

3. *Manner of Gauguin.* Gauguin worked in very limited space, almost a flat pattern in simplified color.

4. *Manner of Picasso* (1910). Analytical Cubism presented many spatial aspects of objects simultaneously.

5. *Manner of Severini.* The Futurists repeated parts of objects seen consecutively, to approximate movement.

6. *Manner of Braque* (Collage). Actual applied objects of varying textures create space through overlapping planes.

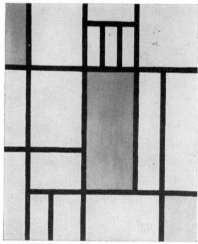

7. *Manner of Dali.* Surrealism usually suggests unlimited distance rather than creative pictorial space.

8. *Manner of Mondrian.* Mondrian's space is two-dimensional, with limited space suggested by color.

Compressed Space

Space is compressed in this diagram in several ways, volumes having been flattened by avoiding space-describing elliptical shapes, which are replaced either by circles seen from above or by straight lines in front view.

In addition, verticals and horizontals flatten the diagram by repeating format lines where diagonal or converging lines might otherwise indicate deep space.

To further reduce space, lines in differing spatial planes have been linked as one, as in the line to the jug from the base of the bottle, and where the bottle label connects with the two planes behind. But even so, there is still a limited spatial recession shown in the above diagram.

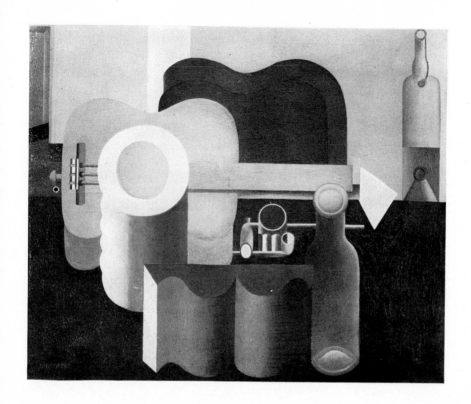

Compressed Space

The use of two vantage points in this picture helps to reduce space as does the subjective linking of foreground and background. Implied lines connect both the near bottle and vertical moulding edge with the guitar in the background plane.

LE CORBUSIER (CHARLES ÉDOUARD JEANNERET): Still Life. *Collection of the Museum of Modern Art, New York.*

Compressed Space

The figures and animals in this picture are indicated by planes without volume, which allows them to be compressed on the picture plane, but, in overlapping, to also express limited space.

Indian Rajput: The Hour of Cowdust. *Museum of Fine Arts, Boston, Mass.*

Compressed Space

Reversed perspective, flat textural pattern, multiple vantage points, transparency, and planes without volume all contribute to the space compression in the organization of this picture.

PABLO PICASSO: Still Life. *Courtesy of the Art Institute of Chicago.*

Reversal of Perspective

Since converging lines in mechanical perspective will give the illusion of distance, a reversal of this principle will compress space and bring a composition into closer relation with the picture plane.

Reversal of Perspective

This composition is flattened by the progressive *increase* in size of the figures and pathway on the left, which reverses the apparent diminishing-size relationships of mechanical perspective.

MASSIMO CAMPIGLI: The Orphan School. *Virginia Museum of Fine Arts, Richmond, Virginia.*

Reversal of Perspective

The table top in this picture is compressed in space by reversed perspective, while the vertical lines in the lower left also help to flatten the picture.

JAMES LECHAY: Gold Fish. *Photograph courtesy of the Macbeth Gallery.*

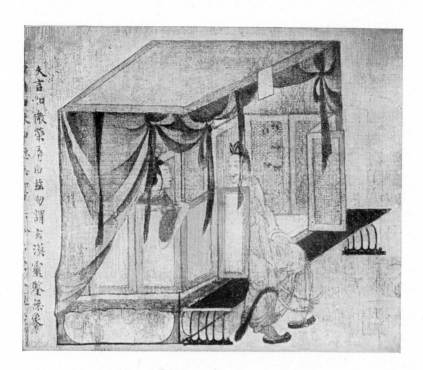

Reversal of Perspective

The Chinese used reverse perspective as far back as the fourth century; and although they have long known of mechanical perspective, they have preferred to show recession by lines which *do not* converge.

Ku K'ai Chih: Chinese Painting (Fourth Century). *British Museum.*

Transparency and Interpenetration

Transparency and interpenetration in painting are an extension of vision, "seeing through" forms, and indicating differing spatial positions at the same time.

In the above diagram, the upper gray plane can be seen either in front of the bottle or behind it in space.

Transparency and Interpenetration

In this still life, the tall rectangular plane in the left foreground will appear to be vertical on the picture plane at one moment and will recede in space in the next. Due primarily to its transparent and interpenetrating quality, the fluctuation of this plane combines both flat pattern and pictorial space.

GEORGES BRAQUE: L'Atelier. *Courtesy of the Rosenberg Galleries.*

Pattern Combined with Space

This diagram is a simple illustration of one of many methods for combining flat pattern with pictorial space.

The left side of the receding rectangle is a *space* line, but while the right side of this rectangle also appears to recede, it does so only from its relation to the space line on the left. In itself, it is a vertical, without space, and is subjectively linked with the top and bottom of the format as a *flat-pattern* line on the picture plane. It is only in combination with the *space* line on the left that this pattern line also expresses space.

Pattern Combined with Space

This picture is very similar in space-pattern combination to the preceding diagram. Space is established on the left, but the vertical pattern-space line is subjective, an implied line of collective smaller directions which carry directly down from the vertical post in the upper right through the figure to the fruit at the lower edge of the format.

PAUL GAUGUIN: Seated Woman. *Courtesy of the Worcester Art Museum.*

Pattern Combined with Space

Here, again, is a similar combination, with a space line at the left and a more pronounced but still subjective line down the center of the picture.

JAN MABUSE: Christ at the Home of Simon. *Brussels Royal Museum.*

Pattern Combined with Space

Matisse has used a line which is in vertical space in the upper section of the picture, while the lower half recedes, the two combining in one space-pattern direction in relation to the space line on the left.

Henri Matisse: The Moorish Screen. *Photograph courtesy of the Information Division, French Embassy.*

EQUIVOCAL

SPACE

Equivocal Space

In the diagram on the left, the positions in space of the two still-life objects are clearly established, both by relative position and by overlapping planes. But all spatial positions in the second diagram are not fixed, for the jug will continually fluctuate in space from far to near. This fluctuation is caused by *equivocal space,* or space that can be seen in two ways at the same time; in this case the cause is the dual contour which describes parts of both objects at the same time.

The right hand diagram also demonstrates another kind of equivocal space, where the dark foreground plane unites with the dark plane of the jug, again forming *two* planes which can also be seen as one.

Equivocal Space

The equivocal space in the above picture is similar to the variety described in the last paragraph on the preceding page.

In this picture, the dark shape of the near central figure continues up into the composition as one unbroken plane, flat on the surface of the picture, or may be seen as part of each three successive planes in space.

Aquiles Badi: Spanish Café. *Study collection of the Museum of Modern Art, New York.*

Equivocal Space

The exact position in space of the hand against the profile of the face, as well as that of the profile itself, are equivocal in that the dual contour (with no overlapping planes) will not establish a definite spatial position.

Pablo Picasso: Seated Woman. *Collection of Mr. and Mrs. Lee A. Ault.*

Equivocal Space

Space in this picture is equivocal where the angle of the far bridge continues down the back of the leaning figure. Background and foreground are thus linked by *one* line common to forms on *two* planes in space.

EUGENE BERMAN: Venise, Le Pont. *Photograph courtesy Julien Levy Gallery.*

Equivocal Space

In this detail from Fra Angelico's *Annunciation*, space is equivocal where the flowing line of drapery descends from the shoulders to cross the figure and link up with the right side of the distant door. This tying together creates a *new* plane, part figure, part wall, which fluctuates between the two dimensions in space.

Equivocal Space

There is also another equivocal use of space in this picture, where the line of the far side of the stool continues across the figure to the floor of the distant doorway.

FRA ANGELICO (1387-1455): Annunciation (Detail). *Museo di San Marco, Florence.*

SKETCHES AND

FINISHED PICTURES

Nicolas Poussin

In this preliminary sketch for the painting on the opposite page, the dark interval is basically abstract, for the dark shapes are *first of all rhythmic directions in the composition* and only secondarily descriptive of individual figures.

Rape of the Sabine Women

The dark interval in the final painting is not as heavily accented as in the sketch, while the background buildings have been enlarged and brought into a more satisfactory pattern and space relationship.

NICOLAS POUSSIN: Rape of the Sabine Women. *Louvre.*

Vincent van Gogh

These two pictures represent different versions of the same subject (in two mediums) rather than being a preliminary sketch and finished picture, a difference in technical method rather than in composition.

VINCENT VAN GOGH: Cypresses by Moonlight. *Courtesy of Oxford University Press, New York, and Phaidon Press, Vienna.*

The Starry Night

The values in the painting are more solid and opaque than in the opposite linear treatment, due mainly to the difference of medium.

Georges Seurat

This is one of several preliminary sketches Seurat made for the picture opposite; but while he followed the sketch, the artist continued to make changes during the development of the final picture.

Afternoon on Grande Jatte Island

The completed composition follows the sketch to a great extent, but the dark and light contrasts are stronger and much more concise.

GEORGES SEURAT: Afternoon on Grande Jatte Island. *Courtesy of the Art Institute of Chicago, Helen Birch Bartlett Memorial Collection.*

José Clemente Orozco

Some painters *begin* their compositions in tone values, combining value and form at the same time, while others, as in this working drawing, start with line and add values later.

José Clemente Orozco: Preliminary Sketch for Wives of the Workers.

Wives of the Workers

Converting a *line* drawing into tone presents new problems, for variations in tone create new shapes not possible to foresee in a purely linear design.

In Orozco's completed fresco, note how important the added dark value in the sky becomes in accenting the receding wall's direction. But even more significant is the change in *drawing* of the woman holding the child, a change which affects the entire picture.

José Clemente Orozco: Wives of the Workers. *National Preparatory School, Mexico City.*

Dong Kingman

Dong Kingman does not make preliminary sketches for his water colors, but in painting from nature leaves certain areas blank to be later integrated in the studio.

DONG KINGMAN: Rain or Shine (First Stage). *Photograph courtesy of the Midtown Galleries.*

Rain or Shine

In carrying a picture to completion, Dong Kingman will often wash
off color already applied to adjust unforeseen developments in the composition. This can be seen where the trees above the automobile have
been removed, and in the lightened street reflections not allowed for in
the picture's initial stage.

Dong Kingman: Rain or Shine. *Photograph courtesy of the Midtown Galleries.*

Alan Reynolds

Here are two paintings, both of which evolved from the same subject matter. While both appear similar, they are each compositions in their own right, relationships of different shapes and textures in differing color areas.

ALAN REYNOLDS: Outbuildings, Pastoral. *Photograph courtesy of the Redfern Gallery, London.*

Alan Reynolds

In the history of art you will often find painters who produce several versions of the same subject. This does not mean that succeeding versions are necessarily better, but only that the artist has later seen new organizational possibilities.

ALAN REYNOLDS: Outbuildings, Pastoral II. *Photograph courtesy of the Redfern Gallery, London.*

Jackson Pollock

Unlike other styles of painting shown in this section, Abstract Expressionism by its very nature precludes any kind of preliminary sketch. This is especially true in the later works of Jackson Pollock. His paint *falls* on the canvas (or on paper, as in the picture shown opposite); how and where it falls depends almost entirely on chance. As new rhythms, patterns, and color effects appear during the painting process, the final creative act consists in knowing exactly when to stop.

To many, Abstract Expressionism is an easy style to imitate; this is an unfortunate assumption, however. Jackson Pollock, himself, was indisputably a mature, fully trained painter *before* he began to paint in this way. Consequently, he was able to take immediate advantage of the accidental effects that evolved during the process of painting. Imitators of the style run the risk of producing paintings that succeed only on a superficial level, since they are not likely to be able to discriminate between the effective and ineffective "accidents."

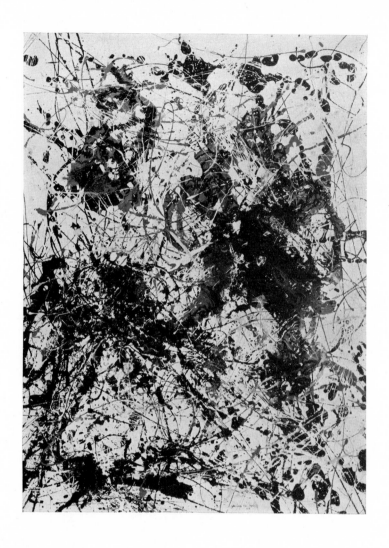

Jackson Pollock: Number 12 (1949). *Collection of the Museum of Modern Art, New York.*

Pablo Picasso

This is one of the later preliminary drawings Picasso made for *Les Demoiselles d'Avignon.*

Les Demoiselles d'Avignon

This painting, composed in 1906-1907 and often called the first Cubist picture, shows the varied influences of El Greco, Cézanne, Matisse, and primitive West African sculpture.

PABLO PICASSO: Les Demoiselles d'Avignon. *Collection of the Museum of Modern Art, New York.*

SPECIALIZED

APPLICATIONS OF

PICTORIAL

COMPOSITION

Composing for Advertising Illustration

Pictures in advertising differ in many ways from painting as fine art, the principal difference being in intention, for a work of art is a complete entity in itself.

But in advertising, a picture is *used* to communicate ideas *outside* the actual picture, a demand for action, the observer entering into what is *going on in the picture*, rather than emotionally experiencing the picture itself. The idea, or subject, is of the utmost importance in advertising illustration (not true in the fine arts), for if the advertising picture appears as a substitute for reality, it may have solved its particular problem. In advertising, the picture can be incomplete (needing words to complete the idea), can be poorly designed (as a copy of nature), can have a useful life of only one second in time, and can still be a successful advertising illustration. But it can seldom give to the observer the personal feeling of the artist (as does a work of fine art), for advertising drawings are not usually the work of one man but of several, and the subject and arrangement are usually prescribed before the final picture is even started.

There are different *opinions* about the use of fine art (easel pictures) in advertising, but the works of painters turned advertising illustrators have not, so far, stood very high in the continuing surveys which check advertising readership. The exception to this generality is in certain quality advertising where the prestige of the fine arts has been borrowed, to be reflected in the product advertised. This category, however, is but a small part of advertising volume. Part of this failure is a misunderstanding, by the painters, of the *illustrative* function of advertising pictures.

Composing for Magazine Illustration

Advertising illustration and magazine illustration, at one time quite separate, are now almost interchangeable; their aims have become similar, with the same illustrators working in both fields.

Illustrations today are intended not only to add to the story they illustrate, but are also used to *persuade* the reader to read the accompanying words. And while the illustrator is necessarily restricted by the details of the story he illustrates, he is still allowed much more freedom than in advertising, where the pictorial arrangement is usually specified. His illustrations, in addition to "selling" the story, are expected to reflect a story's mood, background, and characters, and to express in pictures ideas beyond the limitation of words. Magazine illustrations, like advertising, also have a short life and are usually incomplete away from the words and page for which they were designed.

The question arises, can these two forms of pictorial expression (considered now as one), be made more effective by the inclusion of more principles of composition taken from painting as a fine art? Certain aspects of form distortion must be ruled out in most pictures intended for a mass audience, but no one likes or fully understands a confused, chaotic picture. People seldom recognize the actual use of the picture plane, but will immediately feel the disorder which follows failure to respect it.

But if you ask any advertising man what kind of pictures are most effective in advertising, he will usually reply, "Realistic."

But what makes a picture "realistic"? Certainly not the indiscriminate copying of a fragment of nature, for interest must be accented and directed if any picture is to be generally understood. But aside from any emotional feeling to be gained, pictures in any field will attract and hold interest longer if spatially composed in relation to the format and to the flatness of the picture plant.

"Composing" for Photography

Photography is not an art form in the same sense as painting, but is a scientific medium for instantaneously recording things *already seen*. As a *recording* medium it is without equal, with an authenticity impossible to achieve in any other way. But its limitations should be recognized, for photography which imitates painting is as sterile as painting which imitates a photograph.

A photographer is always free to *select* a subject, but from then on is almost entirely at the mercy of things seen. He may alter his position in space, shift objects in front of his camera, and employ artificial light effects, but his photographic arrangement *must* first exist in the actual world and be seen as an arrangement of some kind *before* the picture is taken. There is no opportunity for later adjustment of forms, as in painting, but only the limited variations in printing and trimming of the final print.

But within photography's limitations there is still a great deal of latitude, for in any picture, no matter how created, lines, shapes, and directions all function in a similar way. But in photography these elements must be recognized *before* the shutter is snapped.

WAYS OF USING

THIS BOOK

Ways of Using This Book

This book describes and illustrates many compositional ideas, not all compatible with one another. The ideas in this book should be considered as tools, to be applied to compositions made in your own way. In studying them, it may be well to make experiments in forms or composition apparently foreign to you, if only to reaffirm your own feelings about the direction your own work should take.

First, you might make experimental compositions of varying subject matter, following the sequence outlined in the book. This would begin with symmetrical composition, on page 44, and continue on through equivocal space. You might equally well select principles at random, skipping about until all sections are covered, for who can say what really comes first in composing any picture?

Another method for study is to make a series of experimental compositions, using the *same* subject matter throughout, somewhat in the manner of the book's diagrams. This plan implies doing the "don'ts" as well as the "do's."

Single qualities in composition have been accented in the diagrams and pictures appearing in most of this book.

But all of these compositions also have other qualities possible to analyze. Why not go through the book with this in mind, isolating these other compositional qualities?

Although pictures recorded through the camera lens must be seen *before* the shutter is snapped, photographers can still experiment with many ideas in this book, in arrangements finally viewed on the *flat* plane of the ground glass. Still-life objects can be adjusted, lighting changed, or vantage points shifted to bring forms from the outside world into closer relationships with each other, and to the picture's format. *Pattern* is more easily controlled in photography than the combination of *pattern* with *space*, so perhaps pattern should be stressed, at the expense of pictorial space. (Remember that pictorial space is not the illusion of distance.)

[236]

The sections of this book outlining *line directions* will, in consequence, be more applicable to photography than the ideas concerning space.

The following are random suggestions for experiments in studying pictorial composition. The order in which they appear is not necessarily the order of importance.

Any medium can be used for experimental compositions—charcoal is easy to change, small pencil sketches are valuable, and pastel is a flexible method for beginning a picture. Thin washes in oil (rather than thick paint) are probably best for starting an oil painting, for establishing the dark pattern of the composition in its early stages.

Varied shapes and textures of colored papers, shifted about by trial and error inside a given format, may evoke imaginative relationships not possible to evolve by drawing alone.

It is an interesting experiment to make *four* pictures from the same composition, turning it four ways, somewhat in the way Lamar Dodd has painted two pictures from one composition. (See pages 12-13.)

As an exercise in color values, make a composition in grays, black, and white, in oil paint. After it has thoroughly dried, paint over it, matching each value with color.

Make an abstract composition of color planes, in oil paint, and put it away to dry. Then make a linear composition (containing subject matter) of the same size and shape, without reference to the previous abstraction. When the abstraction is dry, trace the linear composition on to the abstraction. Then, by the use of transparency and interpenetration, (pages 198-199) combine the subject matter with the abstraction, preserving both in the picture.

This experimental method of composing is valuable for stimulating the imagination within definite restrictions. Two students can work together in this experiment, trading either abstractions or linear drawings.

It is an interesting project to assign the same basic abstraction (without subject) to an entire class, the students to integrate their own subject matter within this basic abstraction. This exercise would be most effective if done *outside* of class, to avoid the influence of one student's work on another.

Compose a *degree of abstraction chart*, similar to the one on pages 118-119, using your own subject matter. This can be done either from a photograph or from a sketch made from nature.

The question often arises, should one draw (or compose) from photographs? The answer is entirely one of attitude, for if a photograph is drawn *from*, interpreted, or used as a spur to the imagination, then by all means use a photograph—but *only* as a starting point, as inspiration, reference or factual information. A slavish *copy* of any photograph can never be more than fragmentary, a lifeless photograph in paint.

Much can be learned by making your own diagrams of the dark (or light) pattern unifying most works of art (similar to the Breughel diagram on page 148). Use a soft black pencil and very thin tracing paper, filling in the dark areas found in reproductions from almost any book on art.

Another diagramming method is to attempt the segregation of *space* and *pattern* lines from one picture, in *two* diagrams. (See pages 200-203.)

There are enough subjects for *composing* pictures within a one-mile radius of where you are (no matter where you are) to last a lifetime. Remember that *your* viewpoint is always more important than anything you may be looking at.

THERE IS NO END

Earlier in this book is an observation on the first objective in composing pictures, the creation of order out of disorder. But order in itself being monotonous, the next step suggested was the addition of variety and *personal feeling*.

Page after page has been devoted to this creation of order and to methods for adding variety to pictures, but very little has been said about the most important element of all, *your personal feeling*. But whether you only look at pictures or actually compose them, it is your own personal feeling that always influences what you see or do.

Remember that someone's personal feeling has given variety to pictures since the beginning of time and will continue to do so in compositions without end.

I would not paint a face, nor brooks nor trees,

> *mere semblance of things, but something more than these.*

I would not play a tune upon the sheng or lute,

> *something that did not sing, meanings that else were mute.*

That art is best which to the soul's range gives no bound,

> *something besides the form, something beyond the sound.*

LI Po

INDEX